REA

W9-CYX-495

ACPL ITEM
DISCARDED

9 1833 02495 2670

811.54 SH9W
SHUMAKER, PEGGY, 1952-
WINGS MOIST FROM THE OTHER
WORLD

Other World

DO NOT REMOVE
CARDS FROM POCKET

ALLEN COUNTY PUBLIC LIBRARY
FORT WAYNE, INDIANA 46802

You may return this book to any agency, branch,
or bookmobile of the Allen County Public Library.

DEMCO

Also by Peggy Shumaker

Poetry

Esperanza's Hair, 1985
The Circle of Totems, 1988

Poetry Chapbook

Braided River, 1993

Wings Moist
from the
Other World

Peggy Shumaker

University of Pittsburgh Press
Pittsburgh • London

The publication of this book is supported by a grant from the Pennsylvania Council on the Arts.

Published by the University of Pittsburgh Press, Pittsburgh, Pa. 15260

Copyright © 1994, Peggy Shumaker

All rights reserved

Manufactured in the United States of America

Printed on acid-free paper

Library of Congress Cataloging-in-Publication Data

Shumaker, Peggy, 1952.
  Wings moist from the other world / Peggy Shumaker.
    p.   cm. —(Pitt Poetry Series)
  ISBN 0-8229-3774-3 (cl.).—ISBN 0-8229-5518-0 (pbk.)
  I. Title.   II. Series.
  PS3569.H778W56   1994   93-37775
  811'.54—dc20   CIP

A CIP catalogue record for this book is available from the British Library.

Eurospan, London

Allen County Public Library
900 Webster Street
PO Box 2270
Fort Wayne, IN 46801-2270

The author and publisher wish to express their grateful acknowledgment to the following publications in which these poems previously appeared: *Alaska Quarterly Review* ("Exit Glacier," "Glacier, Calving," formerly "Kachemak Bay, the Echo," "Hanna Zoe," "Ticking," formerly "Biological Clock," "White Figurehead at Isla Negra"); *American Poetry Review* ("Dust Devil," "How They Are with Each Other, the Woman, the Man," "The Run of Silvers," "Short History of One Hour's Desire," "Three Notes from a Wooden Flute," "Wide Icy River"); *Aurora* ("Creamer's Field"); *Caprice* ("An Intimacy," "Second Childhood: Ashes Off Cabrillo Point"); *College English* ("Bitter Spring," "No Honey in This House"); *The Cream City Review* ("Rapt"); *Cutbank* ("Digging a Garden," "Why Ira Pratt Cocked His Head Like That"); *Hayden's Ferry Review* ("Across the Line," "Hunting Scorpions," "Occupied Territory"); *Iowa Woman* ("Creamer's Field," "Graveyard Shift, 22nd & Tucson Boulevard"); *The James River Review* ("Melt," "Mother's First Words After the Birth, 1952," "Two Rivers"); *Mānoa* ("Ira Pratt's Charts of the Stars," "The Provider"); *New Virginia Review* ("Braided River," "Clitoris"); *Northern Lights* ("Birch Syrup"); *The Northern Review* ("Spawn," "Two Rivers"); *Permafrost* ("Cuentista/Storyteller," "Once You Name It"); *Ploughshares* ("The Day the Leaves Came," "Mask Making," "Strong Stars," "Young Boy Dancing at Playa los Muertos"); *Poet & Critic* ("Passing Through, Passing On," "Ways of Seeing"); *poetryALASKAwomen* ("Braided River," "Three Notes from a Wooden Flute"); *Polar Star* (translations into Russian of "Cuentista/Storyteller" and "Once You Name It"); and *Willow Springs* ("Milagros").

  Most of the Alaskan poems were published in *Braided River,* a limited edition letterpress chapbook from Limner Press, Anchorage, Alaska.

Anthologies:
For a Living: The Poetry of Work ("Graveyard Shift, 22nd & Tucson Boulevard"); *Power Regained: Women Writers at the Turn of the Century* ("Dust Devil," "Rapt," "The Run of Silvers," "Strong Stars"); and *A Thousand Leagues of Blue: Three Centuries of Nature Writing from the Pacific* ("Offerings," "Passing Through, Passing On").

  "Caribou" was December's poem in *1992: A Year of Alaskan Poets,* a calendar produced by First National Bank of Anchorage; Artist Bill Brody made fine art prints using images from "Clitoris" and "Graveyard Shift, 22nd & Tucson Boulevard"; "The Provider" was printed in a limited edition as a letterpress broadside; and "Melt" became an abbreviated kimono form, part of a piece of garment art. (Printing, design, and exhibition by Karla Elling, Mummy Mountain Press, Paradise Valley, Arizona.)

  The author is grateful to the National Endowment for the Arts for a fellowship unfettered by political restrictions and to the peer review panel that selected her work for this honor; to the University of Alaska Fairbanks for its on-going support; and to the many writer friends who gave early drafts careful readings.

Book design by Frank Lehner
Paperback cover and section divider photo by Christine Keith

for Harriet L. Moen

Contents

I

Once You Name It

Once you name it grass,
    the new-mown
    aroma will see you through winter.

Once you name it
    hard durum wheat, it will feed
    the world.

Name it, & you assume
    you can stop looking. Though *snow*
    shows only one facet
    of flake or storm or bank, *powder*
    one quality of the slope
    we're sliding down.

Once you name it Mozart, you expect it
    to save you.

Once you name it
    it's yours. You've claimed it.
    Now you must tend it, watch it grow
    into its name, then grow
    out of its name, come
    into its own.

Once you name it home, it will live in you
    no matter where you live
    no matter how you live
    as long as you live.

Once you name it enemy, you devote your life to it.

Once you name it friend, it will forgive you.

Once you name it love, you begin not to know.

Name it blood, & you see how you're related.
    It thickens, rich pudding
    after death, after birth.

Name it death and you step toward it, just
    as you did before it
    weighed down the tongue,
    melted like a wafer
    or a mouthful of snow.

Once you name it birth, you breathe
    first breath
    and cry, cry
    for the world you've left, harder
    cry, for the world
    you've come to, wide
    awake, helpless, unclothed
    but for your cloak
    of blood, hungry
    to put it to your mouth,
    that whole world
    you've yet to name.

White Figurehead at Isla Negra

Neruda first saw her
cutting through mist, her face
guiding mast and crow's nest,
the infinite rigging
in need of repair.

Chopped up in dry dock, the ship sold
piece by piece, the figurehead locked
in a salt-battered freight house at the pier.
The evening he found her, the wharf lay deserted,
just light enough from the west to turn her

pure white, then gold, ash rose, gray. Neruda knelt
before the locked door, wanting her, whispering
through the keyhole

mango, sangre, mano, cara
mango, blood, hand, face
araña, huerfano, chiste, muerte
spider, orphan, silly joke, death.

Slowly, slowly he made love
to this woman made of wood, slowly
with his mouth he took her in
into himself, where she dances
yes today over his swells and breakers
through his squalls and still waters.

Her aroma of barnacles and split timber
never mellowed, even after years on land.
The soldiers who flooded the stone house
on Isla Negra took it with them,

forever on their hands. They crushed delicate
ears of seashells, smashed cities
of odd bottles, chipped
mosaics of fishes and tiled faces
of the sun. The figurehead floated
in a thousand splinters,
rode the rising
crest of the tortured river, forced
churning through the house.

And the water could not help behaving
like water. Held back, it broke out
more vicious than before, breaking down
the stone house on Isla Negra, stirring up
killing muds, the swamp of great sorrow.

Neruda died heartsick, hearing
helicopters drop flames on his nation's
dreams. Thousands of
mourners gathered like storm clouds.

The soldiers, muscles aching,
licked their lips, and tasted salt.

Young Boy Dancing at Playa los Muertos

Had he been naked
as he skipped
shivering
out of the waves
we would not have known
he was so poor.

But he was not
naked. He wore
around his hips
an exhausted
pair of cast-off
underwear
gathered up at the hip,
secured
with the wire twist
from some tourist's
loaf of bread.

He shivered,
the edges of his lips
blue as the Virgin's veil.
Semana Santa, Holy Week, too early
really for perfect swimming.
Vendors hawked
Taxco silver, mangoes
on a stick, onyx seahorses
chiming, whole perch
skewered and seared.
His eyes swam after
the fish boy.

Timbales called out the guitarrón—
mariachis knocked Norteño beats
blanket to blanket up the beach.
The skinny one held on to his saggy
pants, elbowed close to sing along.
Someone else's fat papá lifted an eyebrow
in invitation, laughed, and together
man and boy danced a slick merengue,
flicked their hips ta-ta-ta,
swirled, one hand
suave against the belly,
the other a green rooster
kikiriki-ki
sunrise all day long!

The boy's whole body
told its truth—
he was not starving, no matter
what his ribs said. And his skin
could go ahead and offer the opinions
of its array of scars—no slash,
no welt, no still-healing burn
along his face, neck, shoulder
could talk louder
than the genius of his tiny
hips, those quick and playful
acts of God.

Being Fed

Houston, 12–31–92

I brought you lentils and curry
and the rich red grapefruits
. Texans call rubies.

A containership rammed a barge
loaded with sulphur. It cracked
in half and the center sank,

two jagged ramps jamming the channel
and who knows what
under the surface.

On movie screens all over Houston
(America, the industrialized world)
genies were given their freedom.

Heavy fog.
The last night of the year.
I longed to talk with my mother

about nothing at all, small
matters, a joke only she
would understand.

That evening your boss said
you had to go to the hearings, listen
to the ship's pilots, the tug captain.

Men wide as refrigerators
guaranteed rice and bullets
for stick-limbed Somalis.

Flies on their eye crusts
examined the scene
from every angle.

In the spice aisle at Fiesta
I wandered among tastes
foreign, exotic, everyday.

Those we savored, those we
never touched to our tongues.
Who puts this to her mouth?

Midnight count,
how many places could I
feel your heartbeat?

A woman in Bosnia
for fear it too would be lost
had to remove

her ring. It slipped off
without touching her knuckle,
worn yoke lifted from

a bone-sharp mare.
She folded her hands, prayed
for the worst

to be over. Two world
wars, a survivor,
she never dreamed

this. All the young ones
sent off, no one
says where.

My mother, for reasons she kept
to herself, gave up
twenty years back.

She slipped from this earth
like a fog just thick enough
to keep the view murky.

Her great foghorn laugh
broke to hacks and wheezes.
Wherever breath turns ragged,

uncertain, likely to cause
trouble, that's love.
Without asking

you fed me
red fruit,
your hands so warm.

Strings of firecrackers
blasted Houston a little deeper
in its poison.

A new year.
Stars behind fog, stars
dead long ago. Still shining.

Sanctuary

The jackrabbit's
mapped ears snare their share
of sunset.

Ears set free
heat that would, kept in,
kill . . .

With every breath,
heat inside, deep
inside, Evelia.

Chicken-foot dreams
scratch. She watches kicked dust.
Red desires—that Gabriel's pinned

ankle might heal,
that their daughter's
two languages private on pages

might fly north in Vs,
seasons of berries that bite back.
Silent Evelia, voice of the desert

tortoise, who knows
when to dig in, exactly when
dry earth can again

provide. Her buried
tongue,
a whole life

wanting. Fed children. No
bruises. No need
for what bruises

say.

Gravity

The rigid baby wrapped in rags
is all tucked in. The child amputee

moans softly. The insulated rich
enforce a peculiar quiet,

shushing seismic rumbles
from distended bellies. One day

we will all of us yield
to the attraction of the earth,

the little plots we've left.
Sullied water

seeks its own level
far down and still.

The spirit without a vocabulary
shrieks into the night like patriots

welcomed home.
Somehow we never get around

to talking about it, the pull
to be the quickest draw,

the holster unsnapped always.
It's the code of the West,

stranger. If you're new
to these parts,

listen up. Manifest Destiny
just got an oil change.

We're aimed downhill,
ready to roll, all pumped up.

Decisive Victory

The way the black Lab races for the water
quick as the leash-clip snaps off his collar.

The way the tanager circles above sunbathers.
Jet ski, the way the redhead's straight ponytail whips

as she spins donuts on the water, bucking
her own wake. My God, the way we show off

what we carry inside. Each grain of pollen
a medieval mace, a weapon against breath.

The way we gather our violence, so the explosion
comes across as involuntary. The long way

home. A child strapped to her wheelchair, the way
administrators who have never met her

find cost effective. Clipped grass,
rubble walk, the back way. Rhubarb

in the front yard, the way the inside of a shoe
worn too far wears down the foot,

the inflamed spot spreading, the weight
of our own steps too much to take.

Be Sad

Be sad, dark aureole
    around the unnursed nipple
Sad, la corona
    of the eclipsed eye

Be sad, you neck without a noose

So sad you actually tingle,
    cupped loneliness, the small of the back

Samba in the forest
    of triste
Dance one dance with the one
    whose sadness matches
    your own, the one
    who died before
    you were born,

    the one born long
    after your shoes,
    handed down,
    dance on without you

Sad, sad, sad blood resorbed
    by the hurt eye

Oh world that endures all mirages
    your marrow is sorrow

Bone, tooth, shard,
    puzzle pieces
    apart and flung
    surface later,
    dug up by generations
    who do not remember

Our sadness they pass
        back through their hearts,
        ocean, star,
        earth-old grief
        they reclaim, cherish
        as their very own

Absence of Ocean

And hasn't the sea been lent
for a brief time to the earth?—Neruda

When the sea pulled away
red rocks lifted. Rippled silt
shimmered under an ancient moon.
Then sun. Many days of fierce, dry breath.
Silt made of itself
ten thousand bowls
broken by their own need
to curl up to the other
and know edges
the ocean could never
fathom.

The desert knows
better than anybody
the necessary absence
of ocean. It doesn't ask
it demands
moisture, salt,
the wisdom of each cell.
Each body a body
of water,
restless, stirring, returning
to sky.

Passing Through, Passing On

Waipo'o Falls, Kaua'i

Mist cools the walker's shoulders, hides
half the floating koa.

The red dragonfly drinks
from the still place.

Not afraid to fall, not afraid
of flight, water

repaints air,
earth, light.

Lizard-smooth bottom stones
cradle the swimmer's arch.

Deep water, very cold,
disguises itself with clarity.

Far down Waimea Canyon, the river
stirs red dirt.

Honeycreepers, guardians of canoe makers, call
'elepaio, 'ākepa, 'i'iwi, 'apapane.

These breaths—red tufts of 'ōhi'a,
whistles of the shama thrush.

A child, grown and unsure, listens.
For so many years

she has not heard.
The mother who suffers in this life

speaks from the next
in this place, the last.

Feral pigs hook their tusks
under native roots. Ti falls easily.

At the last moment, the very last
cliff dwellers tuck in their wings.

Silverswords, an Elegy

Haleakalā Crater, Maui

In the time of the large trees
(it has not been long)
good citizens twisted

to prove they were here
taproots, surface roots, hair roots
broke the whole

tangle from cinder dust,
lugged the luminous
globes uphill, cutting

wind dusting their shins orange,
slicing sideways as if
to blow out

the steady flames, white
light alive in the smallest
hairs. It did not take long

to fasten silverswords
all over their half-paid-for
Fords, nor to snap

wavy-edged souvenirs. The extra
weeds they didn't waste. They
lined them up, had a race

to see which one
rolled fastest,
which one deepest down.

Milagros

By the wrought-iron gate of El Tiradito, shrine
to the fallen, to those who will never
get up, a man with no hands
sweeps the dirt yard with dry fronds.
His wrists stop with the abrupt
tidiness of polished stone, rose
quartz, sunlit at the very end.
He calls me hijita, touches my wrist,
accepts a rolled tortilla between his lips.
My guilt, not the guilt of wholeness.
Cactus wood, the soul
weightless and scarred.

Everyone who comes here is broken.
God is broken. We who see
He is broken
draw closer
to Him.

Cuentista/Storyteller

Through the holes in her lobes
she slipped hoops of silver.
Across her breasts, a mist
of wood rose and moss.
She ate skull-shaped
breads spread over tended
graves. Before
the mirror, her mouth O
opened. Another face,
not her own. Her lips
an oval frame.
She loved the face, though it came
to take her life.
The face opened—
another face! She loved
this face, too, and the
one, brown-eyed,
inside its mouth. Each face
held many stories.
She knew them, the light
and the heavy. All the wild
coronas of damp curls,
flaring. She understood
why some people live their whole
lives with their mouths
shut. But she could not.
She spoke their stories.
It was not enough
to keep the blood
inside her body.
Half her blood
burned blue as the ancient

stars. Half her
blood stained the earth
where the healing
herbs flourish.

Mask Making

Broken screen—cicadas drill through
the gauzy scent of orange blossoms
heavy over the grove.
                        One gangly mantis
clambers out of the queen's wreath, kneels
over a jewel-backed beetle.
                        I lie back
on bare tile, my hair
swaddled in threadbare folds
of old towels.
                        The maker
coats my face with a thin clear smear
of Vaseline, cuts strips of
powdered bandage to bridge
chin, brows, lips, nose—dips
into cool water. His fingers strip
white drops from each patch, then tuck
my face in—length by length, a cool
sodden cover *close your eyes now*
his touch assured, reverent,
stay very still until

in the quick desert air
my face lightens, tighter now
and hard. He touches
each crucial place, then lifts
from my cheekbones
another unfinished form

ready for gesso, acrylics,
black feather, bone.

Offerings

Waha'ula Lava Flow, the Big Island

Past twisted girders of the eaten building
past black stone bunting slung
over squared-off cliffs, past
ropy footholds, vast satin folds, jagged
'a'ā brittle and raw

we wander, breathing sulfur, kneeling
to hold a hand for a moment over
molten earth flowing not far
below. For years, the lava opened
around the chosen

stones of the heiau. But now,
the place of sacrifice
lives submerged,
its only marker
a hip-deep stone corral,

still harboring
offerings—a morsel wrapped in ti leaves,
a glinting flask of gin. Behind us,
islands of rain forest rise from the lava,
spared for no reason.

The earth has taken back the black
sand beach, the smooth terrace, the birds'
mountainside. Huge
spumes of acid and steam blast
out of the hissing ocean.

Forces so great leave behind
strands of glass too fine to hold,
leave golden pools of glass
wafers thin as wings
of dragonflies watching.

Ways of Seeing

No filmstrip, slideshow, worksheet, video.
No crib notes. Just swings made of glass—

the elegance of surprise—dangling
chains, new moss, a stream speaking Japanese.

No context, no relief. No right answer
in the back of the book.

Just a giant fern germinating
in the cleft of the 'ōhi'a, fiddleheads,

the tuft inside. Comfort, beauty.
The great justifications. Who can bear

the lover's intensity? Who can bear
not to be seen?

"We have recently discovered
that a woman is not a green pepper,"

one critic notes. Another, "Fat carries
a beneficial connotation

only as a lubricant, and even here,
there is an undertone." We're taught to hate

our very shape, to despise pure sensual
insulation. The foul object,

cask, cuerpo, trunk, chest, storehouse
for wine, for any intoxicant,

planet in orbit, richness of tone, flavor,
sound box, stem, hull, the dissected

locus of learning, object to be destroyed.
Chance and controlled

chance. A virgin rinsing
spinach, believing in choices.

No context. A Colombian cabbie in Miami
takes the long way, asks twice, three

times, nicely, before pulling into an alley.
Or Seattle, a latte cart

outside the welfare office. For solace,
a woman raised in Sonoran desert pictures

horny toads on a glacier.
Edward Hopper, after all, painted meticulously

electrical poles, but never
the superfluous wires.

II

The Provider

for my father

Both arms around your waist, I buried
my face in the cracked black
leather of your jacket. The throaty Harley
leaned too far, throttle
cranked, hot pavement chewing up
our foot pegs.
Any stray patch of gravel
suicide. Scabby saguaro
lurched by, lean and wounded,
never young. You loved

pure speed, that bike, and me,
though I had no way
to see it then.
I was fifteen, amazed
at my body and amazed
at you, all six foot six
shutting down with one look
whistles and hot talk
as we eased blinking
out of the desert
into the Beachcomber,
shut down everybody, then turned

for the first time to look at me
not as your elbow or toe,
there all the time, easy to bump,
but the woman me, the one so far away
I'd left
before you noticed
I could run.

My showing up
slowed you down, made you trade in
your tunes, your bike, your axe—

your life a down payment on mine.
We both got took.
You soured selling Chevys
and office machines. I took care
of the little kids.

Once, I brought a college friend
to your place. Your fourth wife
sang with you, "Bad, Bad Leroy Brown"
and "One Note Samba,"
you clunking along on the clavinet,
those canned drums thumping
like tired pistons.

It was 10:30 in the morning.
A pitcher of salty dogs already
loosened your joints. We sat
on the red velvet overstuff
still shrouded in double-duty plastic.
George Wallace, you said.
The only clear choice. I left.

Father, I am ashamed
how ashamed of you
I've always been, when
I know so little
and that little
learned by leaving.

Your absence
has carved in me a place
that healed like a cactus shoe—
hard, fragile, secret—
the deepest gashes
shelter
for some bounding pack rat
or startled cactus wren.

Hanna Zoe

Mother, because you died
so often

when I was a child
I must go back there

to the crippled mesquite
with your eyes in it

to all the head-on crashes
that did not kill you

to the barbed wire and sand
of your voice, wheezing hard

Don't go too far. You left us
milk money in a can. We left you

under a stone
with no last name, unwilling

to burden you
in death

with your unbearable life.
Who were you then?

Who are you now?
Did you know your father

came to see me
on the night he died

came to my bed and held me,
told me he was going?

36

I had so much to ask
I forgot

to tell him
to touch your face

that way that made you stop
for a moment, in peace.

Mother's First Words After
the Birth, 1952

Because I was her first, no one listened
when my mother cried, "It's time, it's coming!"
The nurses patted her hand, crossed their legs,
"We'll tell you, honey, when you're getting close."

So I was almost born between floors, my mother
clamping shut her thighs, some panicky orderly
pinning her shoulders to the gurney. My father,
a lanky teenager dreaming of a shovel-head Harley

with a suicide clutch, paced.
When we were mopped up,
presentable, he slouched in, reached afraid
to touch my mother's flattened, baby-fine hair.

His hands felt enormous, charming, full
of forgiveness. Face to the wall, my mother spoke
from far away. "I'm sorry
it isn't a boy for you, honey."

Hunting Scorpions

The parents were both alive then,
no divorce,
so we spent cool November
hunting scorpions in the Rincons,

turning rocks with our sneaker toes, checking
with twisted off greasewood switches
first the darker upturned faces of stone,
then the sandy rock shallows. We whisked

fuzzy seedpods over the moistness,
hunting the striped or tan
little hook of poison
curled over. We'd scoop them up

into Dixie cups and walk them
level back to camp,
back to the circle of rock we'd set
hemming in paper plates and dry mesquite

that gave us back
our fingers, chilled to curls.
The scorpions would scramble
against steep daffodils

waxing the sides of the cup,
so we'd calm them with a glug
or two of beer. Once Gin
floated hers, damn near got stung

before it drowned. Mostly, we
squished the soppy cup between two
firepit rocks, and watched.
Most of the beer left

in a huff. The scorpion
caught a clawhold on the seam
and clambered up.
    For a moment, it wavered, twitching,

then the edge of the cup
clenched in on itself, petals
pressing back to the bulb,
the trapped one ticking inside.

Dust Devil

Tucson

On this dry earth, forgiveness glides
like a cloud shadow

passing over a desert school yard
erasing the ragged shade
thrown by the palm frond ramada—

the almost-moist kiss of coolness
on a day so hot
the tetherball hangs
sticky and soft
at the end of its rope.

The girl on the fringe for dodgeball
stops, raises her face
to the blessing of this tempered sun,

soothing, welcome, nearly wet
in a place where water's always holy.

The whole world's lifted
grain by grain, each point sharpened
then pointed here,
now.

Gritty wind picks up,
whipped wind whirls—
all the boys corral their faces
in the crooks of their elbows
all the girls squat on parched heels
holding skirts down to shield
slick calves from mean sand stings.

Dust lifts itself up to the sky.

The girl rinses her eyes,
blinking above the drinking fountain's
leaping arc, turns

and is chosen—Blindfolded, she's
twirled, told *You're It*, then left
to stumble dizzy, hands outstretched

toward the sound of breathing
just out of reach, the child knowing
everyone else is running, everyone else can see . . .

The sun's back out. Her closed eyelids glow
red as veined petals
of tulips held to light, tulips
she swiped from the flickering altar
at the feet of the Virgin
Our Mother of Sorrows, forced

blossoms, waxy offerings
lifted from someone else's God
on a dare.

Second Childhood: Ashes
Off Cabrillo Point

for my uncle, Daniel George Moen
April 1, 1939–October 3, 1988

Helpless before helplessness, you shied
from wheelchairs, stutterers, any limp or cough.
You finished sentences even for those who could talk,
your flawless daughters, your dynamite wife.

More than once and too loud you announced
brash in your young bull's bravado,
"If I ever get like that,
I hope you shoot me."

Like that, legs and arms drawn up from disuse,
your hard-gripping hands flailing behind bars.
Nine years since your wife's CPR kept you breathing,
nine years since the ambulance slammed shut, screaming,

brought you up heart-stopped to the first
intensive ward. You began to grow younger
as we agonized and signed for someone else
to pull the plug. Younger, beyond language,

your baby-squall lungs sang their racked songs.
Deaf like always, you did what you weren't supposed to:
Woke. Heard. Spoke. Cursed. Cried. Watched
the life you'd made take off and leave you.

Understood, sometimes, small portions of your loss.
After a while, you stopped screaming.
Suffered quietly each time we had to tell you
the long-ago deaths of your father and sister.

We fed you apple-spice yogurt, fresh lefse,
black licorice, beer. Ran with you down the scorched
canyons of your childhood. You stood on the rim,
flicking lighted matches in, seeing how far

how far before the wind snagged them or they
        fluttered out,
but one caught faster than breath, ripped
brush and scrub in a blinding flash, the left side
seared, the waste beyond reckoning.

You ask if we think someday you'll have
        what it takes
to get married. We tell you again *Whitney Lynn,*
William Daniel, the names of your grandchildren.
This much you've got by heart:

triple-tonguing "The Trumpeter's Lullaby,"
you take the stage for graduation, solo.
Your mother need no longer suffer
her nightmare of leaving you untended.

No Honey in This House

I had no sooner moved in
than the morning turned black
with them. Their vicious hum.
Six million hairy legs
clamped to my screen—
peering through, I
watched them swarm
the small mimosa,
coating it, a live
demented fur.

No provisions
in this new place—just spices
carted over from the old house.
Together, we fasted—the drones
clustering the swollen queen,
no combs or chambers yet.

Without serum or shield, I called
downtown, sure that a keeper in a veiled hat
could lure them, prod them, smoke them
off the overloaded branches into drawers
of those white file cabinets.

He'd cart them to the edge of a farmer's ditch
where they'd count out their days
over alfalfa, zucchini, tangerines.

But outside the voice cried
Close your windows. Sit tight.
I heard the hisses of a sinister
compression, tasted the foul mist
powdering the air. A poisoned hush
lay down among us. Rakes and shovels
tidied the fallen into plastic.

The mimosa lay broken
too far down to prune. I mourned
her petals' sheer wash of magenta,
her leaves' feathering of an evening.
Free to go, I sat cloistered
watching tiny wingéd meteorites
catch light for the briefest of instants.

Bitter Spring

The earth here is surprised again
that the seed is not satisfied
to stay covered so smoothly

but must work its way out
like a Chinese courtesan
loosening the drawstring

on the silk bag encasing her,
the bag that suffered with her
the beating intended to exact

precisely one life's ransom.
Not yet not-husband, not-wife,
we squint like convalescents

prematurely released. Make love to me
like always
leave me alone.

Graveyard Shift, 22nd
& Tucson Boulevard

Most nights, I liked the place
fine. No schedule, no calls, no
supervisor upping some unreal
quota of keystrokes.
All I had to do was scrub floors,
stock shelves, make a little
change. No sweat.

Circle K had some
arrangement—for stores
close to the railroad,
extra patrols.

It was slow. Two cops
rousted the wino with the purple
bandanna, shoved him
hurtling across the tracks.

I checked the level
on the unleaded, shivering.
Thawed my fingers around a cup
so black I saw myself, haloed
in a strange neon moon.

I thought of the girls, asleep.
Finally, we had our own place.
No matter what,
they couldn't answer the door unless
they knew the voice.
Wished I could call. I bent

for an armload of Kent and Pall Mall,
heard the front doors scrape. *Wipe your
feet* I hollered. Wasn't a regular. He
wandered over by the back. I bent
again, then straightened halfway,
my eye catching
movement by the register.

He was turned away. *Hey,
you can't come back here.*
It was the voice
I'd use on children, firm. He turned,
hefted a smooth, face-sized
river stone and chanted

    *I'll bash
    your fucking head in.*

We stood like that, his face
bloated and shaking. His shirttail
out and ripped. *Take anything
you want.* Up, up, up,
bent elbows, the stone rose
two-handed over his head,
then down
        and down
                and down

Occupied Territory

He reaches to the end
of his fingertips and touches
the splintered side
of an abandoned house.

No furniture, no drapes,
just the unfaded patches
pictures once covered:

infant, seashore,
mother, warrior.

Two boards with nails pried loose
boost him—a deep sill
receives his elbows, his breath
a circle of light. Inside

an unveiled woman
dances to the strains of a green piano,
its keyboard open and oiled.

Her lover peppers
a choice delicacy, made from scratch:
his padded mitts hold out

a hot covered dish.
                        He cautions
his love not to lift the lid.
When she does, the aroma
of a fine wild stew steams
her face.
                        In the dish

not one hangnail mars
his exquisite patchwork
of hands, some calloused,
some grasping,
                some still clenched.

Why Ira Pratt Cocked
His Head Like That

Twelve hours a day, six days a week.
Stamping out barrel staves, cattle tanks,
strongboxes, silo sheeting. At first his brain
swelled, slamming all night the same
steel chants, his bones jamming, misaligned.
They bought real glass for the windows.

A dropped sheet 4 x 8 sliced off two toes.
The straw boss didn't dock him.
Ira walked tighter, repaired his own shoe.
God preserve us from what we get used to.
They paid the improvement on the home place.

The knocking in his head slacked off, and he slept.
*Couldn't startle him if you drove a buckboard
through the bed.* He liked Amy saying that.
The day after Easter, he rose early,
checked the nest. Watched newly hatched robins
open their beaks. Then his hands began to sweat.

Ira Pratt's Charts of the Stars

Open your eyes, Zoe.

Mars closes in tonight,
easing over by Aldebaran.
Don't be fooled—it's easy
to mistake them. Both glow red
but Mars stays steady.

Zoe, when I look at the night sky I think
of beings more lonely than we are,
of the ancients whose pictures we still see
up there, and the shepherds who needed them to be.

Remember when Scorpio went
to sting Orion? The archer's past
danger now, shooting his arrows west.
Or maybe the scorpion hides
on over the earth's ledge,
past our vision's reach.

Libra has grown very dim,
hard to find. What we've agreed to see
may not show up this time.
But Libra's there. And it's healthy, Zoe,
to reserve love for what you can't be sure of.
Every turn of the earth
speaks a new good-bye.
The going on was never rare.
We just live here, now, through
small guilts and large longings—

and when we *see*, staring past the healed bone
still hurting in winter, when we
see what *is*, not what we've been told,

it's a shelter, Zoe, to stand under,
to understand, this seeing
this being
twice alive.

III

The Day the Leaves Came

For so long the hillside shone white,
the white of white branches laden, the sky
more white, the river unmoved.

And when the first stirrings started
underneath, the hollowing subtle,
unpredictable, rotten crust gave way—

ice water up to the ankle! She
turned from her work and shook
her wet foot. The buds had broken.

Not the green of birches in full leaf.
Not meadow, tundra, berry patch, tussock.
For this moment only, this green—

the touch of one loved
in secret, a gasp held in,
let go.

Rapt

Glazed aspen, low sun, snag branches
snowed over except
where eagles choose to rest.
One jangles her head—neck

feathers splay, troubled and wrung.
She sneezes, then preens
tucking white over brown
lifts off, weightless,

catching the perfect surge, kicking
back a burst of white off laden
boughs, skimming
low over the vast

open river, the last in Alaska, wide Chilkat
running warm in December. A choir
of her sisters swivels
to watch.

Whoom, whoom, she's fast along the surface,
the inner curve of her wings filling
with light. Feet first, talons
flick-snatch a flap of silver

from the river. She lifts and banks,
someone screes. Not five feet
from me, she lands, spreading
her catch lengthwise

along the branch. Her claws
pin it still gasping—
her sharp beak
punctures. Liquid bites, chlap, chlap

so close I hear them
drip, hear the wet rip
as fish muscle turns
into eagle. What's not eaten

shivers, ripples. Slippery entrails spill,
shimmer over the limb. Iced
cottonwoods creak. Grainy wind
lifts sun-sparked snow. She glances

my way
without concern, her yellow
eyes intent. I shake
my head and feel

what has been wind-torn
mend.

Ticking

My doctor, Clarice, says if I want
        to have children, I better
        get to it.
        I have a lumpy right breast.

I wash my face with the corner
        of a fresh towel
        moistened from the jug
        kept to prime the pump.

I could go out now to shovel
        snow while snow
        is still
        falling.

Camp robber jays jeer on the porch rail.
        February redpolls
        flit through
        snow for the seed they know
        is there.

On the table, a glass sphere,
        the splay of stems—
        hothouse iris, fuchsia,
        tiger lily, the furls
        fragrant, open.

I have never loved innocently,
        but I have loved
        purely, often.

What child could bear me?

The Run of Silvers

If, inside me,
his one cell swam among millions
as if it knew the way,
met the ripe star falling
through my thick clouded sky

then plunged in headlong
renouncing even the tail that allowed it
to make the swim,

then I will tell our new
daughter or son, the one
taking shape, taking over
inside and out
that one afternoon

a run of silvers surged
through Resurrection Bay,
such hurry toward death!
Their potent ballet—muscular
dazzling leaps into the blinding
sparkle of an air they can't breathe—

how they hovered
in blue air—angels, perhaps,
messengers surely

sent to nourish and teach
those of us who might listen . . .

They did not know where
they were going,
they simply found their way.

We did not catch our supper that day.
Glacial spray from the crashing falls
chilled our faces, cleared our eyes.

In never-ending daylight
sea otters rocked
belly up on the incoming
tide, swallowing whole
blue mussels
stone pounded
against their chests.

We never had touched each other
in quite such tender danger.

Caribou

Hoof—
    one hoof
        enters powder, sinks
           through fresh snow

touches,
    breaks
        the light crust
          pushing deeper

to hard pack. Haunch deep.
    Only then
        can she
          move on.

The change we
    need so delicate
        so crucial

it might be
    silent, it might
        be this quiet
          step, breath.

Braided River

Under the ice, burbot glide
as if giving birth
to silence.

Someone who held the auger straight
drilled clean through
to moving water,

set gear, then hurried home,
chilled blood pulling back
from the surface, circling deeper

toward the center, the sacred.
As all winter the heartwood
holds the gathered birch sap

still. Ours is only one bend
of a wild, braided river.

Glacier, Calving

Kachemak Bay, Alaska

We picked through shoulder high
wide blade grasses, listening to the fading
snicker and he-yup of the trainer
posting a skittish foal. The massive
hooves of unshod Morgans turned the soil,
carved hollows to catch timothy seed,
grave half-moons to cradle rain.

A sweet-water stream emptied across rock beach
into Kachemak Bay. Across the way, glaciers
thrust splintered shale into black-shined
moraine, quick rivers charging inside them.
The bay caught the light, threw it back.

Something inside you let go.
You spoke of your father, who never learned to read,
grinding his teeth as you helped his hand
scrawl the letters of his painful name.
You told of the grandmother who wished you
never born, for fear you'd be like him. I held you.
That bitter river coursed.

At sunset we hiked to the rough lumber cabin.
Mud daubers under the eaves
dove for our faces, then banked
and soared over the unfenced field.
All night mosquitos drilled through sleep—

each slap of little death
awake, and wet, and echoing.

Three Notes from a Wooden Flute

A moon with two points
cradles chill mist.
Where you are,
                    can you see it?

Moist starlight on new moss—
flannel blue, a melting
snow ridge

I care for this birch bud
so tightly wrapped
in itself
it seems solid

One passing shadow,
        a trickle at the root,
a hush of breath
        along the unclothed limb—

it will somehow know
        to open

Two Rivers

On a day I spent wondering
if I were two weeks pregnant

the stable hand guessed high
on my weight, but led out a beauty—

pied rust and white, named Success—
her stirrup hit me in the chest.

Straining to pull up, I spooked her
but calmed us both by stroking

her broad, supple haunch.
All mounted, we crossed the wet meadow,

Success kicked into a sudden canter—
white water! no raft!

I didn't capsize, just felt
my body begin to remember

power, turned by the slightest
suggestion of rein or knee.

Later, among birch tending to gold
I began to list, the saddle

edging sideways step
by step. I slid

laughing to the sodden leaf-pack,
watched my friend

persuade the mare
with a knee to the belly—

stop pooching! then cinch
the strap up tight.

I felt it all, her urge
to gnash weeds into green foam,

the insult of the bit,
her quickening

when the trees parted
and the rainwashed air moved by.

Creamer's Field

Half-gold leaves abandon the birch.
Very soon frost heaves will shuck
great curls of road off the ridge.
The earth will harden, even the air
turn stiff.

This stubbled field of barley
very soon will pull down deep into itself
all witness of the season's planting,
harvest, grazing—even this

gray light glinting across vast
swoops of geese—black from far off
but dappled closer, and the fragile, elegant
crooks of sandhill cranes, lifting, settling.

Down rests where they rest, among
ptarmigan and canvasback,
all those languages passing through
one clean morning's air.

Spawn

Biting down, I take into myself
half-frozen herring eggs,
salty pops and crunches

tooth-strained off spruce boughs,
tar-tang of needles
sucked past the chill.

Inside me's their Inside Passage—
they hatch and school, return to spawn
in this milky way—vast briny tingle

of a lifetime's kisses—
all those refused
lingering on the tongue . . .

all those indulged, dissolved,
the sting on the skin, the spiny-edged
kelp-laden surf—

tiny explosions
of lives taken,
given, on each incoming tide.

An Intimacy

Falling
    and already
        fallen

May snow
    lights
        on tufts of moss

dusting
    the bizarre
        upholstery

springing from
    juts and crannies
        broken edges

where the birches'
    many-layered bodies
        have split, scrolled back

and left wide open
    the unblemished
        inner self.

A tinge
    of light-washed pink
        draws one to touch

the translucent ear
    of an infant,
        the open thighs

of a happy woman
    walking
        naked.

Exit Glacier

When we got close enough
we could hear

rivers inside the ice
heaving splits

the groaning of a ledge
about to

calve. Strewn in the moraine
fresh moose sign—

tawny oblong pellets
breaking up

sharp black shale. In one breath
ice and air—

history, the record
of breaking—

prophecy, the warning
of what's yet to break

out from under
four stories

of bone-crushing turquoise,
retreating.

Birch Syrup

As I turned off Spinach Creek Road, I wondered about walking in. In early May, the driveway, a fairly steep quarter-mile dogleg, ran as two small streams split by a mossbacked middle ridge. Caribou lettuce edged the roadway like dusty lace.

The last car in (or out) hadn't sunk too far, so I decided to chance it. First gear—my nimble Honda shinnied up the wet slope, no problem. Sharp left, and I pulled into the turnaround behind the house. Steam rose from an ancient camp stove set up by the cold-storage shed. Glen lifted a hand in greeting, then turned shyly back to his work.

I stretched over the seat for the two fresh baguettes I'd brought from town. Noses exposed, they pointed toward the tall stainless bucket and the steam polishing Glen's ruddy face. Wet spruce and peeling birch stood by, murmuring. A thick sponge of leaves gave softly underfoot.

"Birch syrup," Glen said, adjusting the flame under the clear fluid. He and Melissa had snowshoed to a stand of good-sized white barks, drilled an inch in, and watched the drops gather. They tapped in a short bit of hose, fastened on a pail, and let the warm days and cold nights do their work. In a few clear days, the trees gave seventeen gallons, clean and cold as spring water, with a touch of the tree taste lingering.

Melissa called us in to mince the garlic she'd sprinkle over burbot Glen had pulled up through the ice on the Tanana. We fed each other thin bites of smoked cheese, caught a glimpse of the season's first waxwing, hesitating by the feeder.

Last season a moose offered himself just out the back door. Some people laughed at Glen for taking him—too easy, they said, not sporting. But Glen's Athabaskan relatives told him if the animal leads you on a long chase over hard ground, something's not right in your relationship with the animal. He said thank you, shot it, and forced his kid to stay home that night to help butcher.

A strange dog, cocoa brown and bounding, tagged along on our after-dinner walk, running ahead to bite the snow, running back when we moseyed too slowly. Perfect ovals of stone caught Melissa's quilter's eye. She chose a smooth black one to hand to me.

The whole watershed—mountain, hillside, valley, flatland. Each rise balanced with a hollow, and every-thing alive, connected.

The sap had boiled down to dark amber. We strained it into boiled jars, hand-tightened the lids. I stayed too long, almost till dark in a time when darkness almost doesn't come. They gave me a jar to take home.

Melt

Sun-warmed cedar planks—
      the scent of spruce and peeling birch—
        your mouth finds mine, we turn

from the porch rail
      to take this journey of tongues—
        a shiver of moisture

the natural spring
      rainwater under snow
        a shimmer in the hollow.

Digging a Garden

I rake back, twice, this new place,
once to clear leaves—the fan-teeth
tinging ancient songs, one note for each
catch along this patch
of earth's holy music-roll.
Then the law-and-order jags of a straight rake
straining to uproot grass so crabby it would argue
even about the sureness of death, holding on
as if possession were enough,
as if roots and prior claim
could hold sway.

A light mist settles as I break earth,
a benediction cooling my throbbing face,
softening the soil. I rise, a dream
in a stranger's sleep, away from the hovering
magnolia, out of the radius of pine straw
to this corner, exposed.

Chard, onion, squash, beans,
staked and braided plum tomatoes.
This is one version of the future. For now,
my right arm, muscles awake and complaining,
lifts rounds of soil up, out, and over
row after row, turning what has seen light
back to face the under-earth, turning up
this white chrysalis, some creature
learning within its confines how to fly.

Under the overhang of old shrub,
strawberry runners deepen to red,
stemming each span of the unknown
with three possibilities. Two paces

distant, a pearl gray mockingbird
trimmed with black wing bands
keeps pace—fearless, taking in
translucent earthworms amazed
to find themselves suddenly
turning up
in this world.

Turned up or turned out
some burrow back to the familiar.
Others, consumed, take flight.

Strong Stars

Mottled grouse peck
    up gizzard stones
        before the first snow—

seasons move on
    as if the human heart were not
        infinitely fragile.

The sow bear's stained snout lifts,
    sniffs the wind, then bows
        to claws raking in

stems, berries, rasping leaves.
    A twelve year old, pleased, tells her aunt
        I kissed a boy four times and my tooth

grew back in.
    Beside the barrow ditch, the bandy-legged fox
        bounds into finger-thin willow.

Strong stars surround the green
    wash of the aurora, God's love, the moisture
        of a woman's orgasm . . .

From here, we can see much farther
    than we can walk.
        We walk to the edges of our bodies.

IV

How They Are with Each Other, the Woman, the Man

They passed between them the huge
green coconut it took two hands to hold,
its skin smooth and cold against their palms.
They sipped up the milk, icy and blue,
through a pink straw, shaking out the last
drops on the sand so they could hurry
back to the man with the machete.

One whack and the cool world
opened like every sacred hollow
to offer more
of what they never knew
they wanted. The vendor splintered off
a thin curve of shell—rude spoon
to scoop out the creamy gel,
swirl it with salt, lemon,
chili, lift it to the tongue—

All morning their quarrels had circled—jagged
wings of frigate birds, prehistoric,
their great split tails
open Vs—no victory,
no peace. Spread legs. The impossibility
of blue. The woman.

The man. Each craving. They floated
in salt, ancient.
Not speaking. Pelicans rattled,
flung shattered water from their furry
heads. The woman, the man. Broken
waves, dream's hymen, bitter vow.

Green coconut, green
the punctured roundness
that slakes the body's
great thirst, green

the split husks
that invite us in,
the woman, the man
to the soul's
immense hunger

under
the sun's life-giving
cancerous grace.

Across the Line

Tucson/Nogales

For a few days in August we returned together
to places we'd loved separately, long before

I eased myself onto you, facing away,
so inside you felt a silky backwardness.

Our bellies ripe and dripping, tender wedges
of cantaloupe feeding each other . . .

We drove south to a country where aromas alone
called us in off the street. A roadside

vendor squeezed green lemons over a gordita,
the meat shine sticking with us even after sucking.

We asked the way to the Cavern, long since
burned and no longer serving

tequila with a worm
or the soup of turtles.

You dropped folding money in the paper cup
of the high-cheeked woman

wrapping God's eyes
around twigs of the velvet mesquite.

La Sirena, heavy breasts above the waterline,
I turned the cards for loteria:

El Diablo, preparing a corner, El Nopal,
prickly paddles studded with thick purple fruit.

To settle the dust, we sucked fibrous paletas
of mango, the sweet chew of piña,

our tongues alive along the frostiness, licking
our fingers, licking

what our fingers held. Thunderclouds
ganged up over Sonoita's wild grasses—

switchblade rumbles of rainwater flashing
dry arroyos, el corazón

shot through, the quick, involuntary
muscle in the chest, the storm

shocking the broken earth,
shaking for the crack of an instant

the certainty of the sky, that storm
pulsing on inside us,

underground rivers swollen, refreshed.

Again, Again

As I'm waking you drift

your stiffening cock

up the back of my knee

Just born as we touch

our new bodies can't wait to laugh

Only for a few reasons,

all holy,

do people kneel

Against my cheek your thighs open

open, wings moist

from the other world

Both my hands, very wet, stroke . . .

Let the mouths be jealous

a little while

You behind me

blind rhino

crashing through brush

I bounce out overripe red flame

grapes for the jays

then wait naked among them

The elegant herons

our long kisses

My nipples between

your teeth—

when the pain turns

exquisite, I fill

your hand

with spring water

Watching me touch

myself you

become a woman

Brace yourself! Bright open lips

swoop down on your kiss

What fine tuning you do, twisting

my nipples, you about ready

in my mouth

After months holding back, you bend

my head forward and nip

the nape of my neck

What deaths do we face

when we refuse

Clitoris

Surely a man named it.

If a woman had chosen, we'd
have hawk tongue, pearl
of flame, olala berry,
suck nubbin, jujube
tsunami.

Wild Iris

All around us
within us

love's secrets
coil below the surface. The part

that will open purple not yet
purple, keeps to itself

color often stolen
(mistaken as vestments, as bruises).

The sacred unfolds
as if all over the world

people terrified and small
got over their certainty, got past

the notion echoing
If you knew me, surely

you would abandon me
leave me again

with my self, alone.
Thawed earth, water moving on.

I want you
to know me.

Wild meadow of secrets
restless underground.

Short History of One Hour's Desire

For the lips of the recording engineer
   moistening each other as the lights bubble up
For the drunken student's breath of cloves
For the staple guns of flamenco heels
For the foreskin slid back over a chewy mushroom
   of oblivion
For the lupus victim carried to her toilet
For the throb of destruction in the baby's temple
For the deaf cartoonist's nodding fist
For the hiker's last switchback before he froze
For the mask-maker's wall of weathered skulls
For oiled springlets on an athlete's brow
For the Russian priest's daughter, her tangles and
   tangles, her hip-length hair
For the composer's fingers stroking
   the businesswoman's ankle
For eyes of the safety patrol who knows
   how hunger hollows bones first
For women skiing cross-country to reach by moonlight
   a place to be naked
For flames centering fine Thai soup
For the singed waitress delivering fried cheese

For the language of touching after long absence
For chicken-scratch dancers under the tamaracks
For molas layering common cloth to brilliance
For the grandmother fading while we go at it raw
For clean incisions on polished clay—water spirit!
For the shapes of animals on our genitals
For the scab's child uncovering a mailbox rattlesnake
For the miracles tortillas wear on their faces
For the hole behind the net
   catching a cancerous neighbor's breath

For the murderer's first child, born retarded
For the little junkie-whore who does not repent
For the racehorse pumped full of painkillers
For the vasectomized man who raises as his own
    his wife's last child
For the man who keeps three wives, and is faithful
    to them all
For the wife nearly ready to have children
For Japanese flags, blood on white tile, no children
For twin obese toddlers moaning for Twinkies
For two fingers sewn back to the drummer's hand
For the split decision of young girls bathing
For the stonewalled wife aiming into concrete
For carpets unvacuumed since he moved out
For the millionaire kneeling to edge his lawn
For the husband grateful beyond questions
    for his wife's return
For the horror of prayers, answered and answered
For the charango, the cuíca, the Día de los Muertos
For shards of flowerpots later mistaken
For the clear-headed moment lust recedes
For musky, bone-shattering novelty
For hundred-year-old letters, uncommitted to the flames
For all the juices we can suck from one another
For the history of one hour's desire

Wide Icy River

How, driving in whiteout
    above tree line the summit
        road washed white blue-white
            gone to swirling powder, we gasp
                whirling inside the frosted sigh

of the earth.
    Straining in whiteout
        our eyes the eyes of creatures
            unsuited to this element
                vestigial, liquid ornaments

splashing for flashes of orange.
    Each marker hovers,
        flicks past too
            fast, we can't let it go we can't
                see it or the next—

beyond our tiny sphere, the expanse—
    white on white, the endless
        domes of our unknowing.
            Our knowing
                what we cannot see

could very well whisk away
    our visible breath.

How the ones we loved
    well enough
        or not
            would miss us with a white-hot
                burning for as long as they

held on. And those who
        held old photographs
                would conjure our voices
                        above tree line, in whiteout,
                                the road drifted over.

Long after the photos
        have fallen, white
                flakes of ash
                        in a stranger's grate,
                                our distant, white-boned

daughter will warm her cold
        ear along the thigh of her lover.
                Her breath on his skin
                        white language
                                he can lose himself in

that white
        on white
                remake us
                        windswept blue
                                in its own image.

Notes

I

"Once You Name It" is for Sam Pereira.

"White Figurehead at Isla Negra": After the assassination of Allende, Pinochet's forces launched a massive campaign of repression and terror in Chile. In spite of their efforts, people gathered to pay their respects to Neruda, risking threats of exile and death.

"Decisive Victory" is for Christianne Balk, and for Karl and Elizabeth Flaccus.

"Be Sad" was inspired by the first part of Vicente Huidobro's *Altazor*.

"Silverswords, an Elegy": Most of the few silverswords that remain on earth are exhibited in exclosures to keep people and animals from disturbing their delicate root systems.

"Cuentista/Storyteller" was inspired by a ritual mask made by El Zarco Guerrero.

"Mask Making" is for Tito Ríos.

"Offerings" is for Frank Stewart and Lisa Erb.

"Ways of Seeing": Lyn Smallwood, "The Trophy Hunter and the Taxidermist," a review of an exhibition culled from the personal collections of Edward Weston and Ansel Adams, in *Seattle Weekly*, 19 June 1991, p. 44. "We have recently discovered, for example, that women are not green peppers—or any other kind of object. Slice off a woman's head and hands and you get a powerful emblem of her physical presence—her sexuality. But you also commit an act of metaphorical violence."

Carla Gottlieb, *Beyond Modern Art*, p. 354. "Fat carries a beneficial connotation only as a lubricant, and even here there is an undertone: oily and greasy are nasty-sounding attributes for the ability to make things work smoothly."

The phrase "object to be destroyed" is the title of a work by Man Ray, first produced in 1923, and accompanied by this advice: "Cut out the eye from a photograph of one who has been loved but is not seen anymore. Attach the eye to the pendulum of a metronome and regulate the weight to suit the tempo desired. With a hammer well-aimed, try to destroy the whole with a single blow."

II

"The Provider" is for John Marshall Howe.

"Hanna Zoe" and "Mother's First Words After the Birth, 1952," are in memory of Hanna Zoe Howe.

"Hunting Scorpions" is for Ginny Draves.

"No Honey in This House" is for Harriet Moen.

"Graveyard Shift: 22nd & Tucson Boulevard" is for Sue Montoya.

"Ira Pratt's Charts of the Stars" is for John and Pamela Howe.

III

"Braided River" is for Hanna Draves.

"Glacier, Calving" is for George Dabney.

"Three Notes from a Wooden Flute" is for Amy Montoya.

"Two Rivers" is for Rick Bass and Elizabeth Hughes Bass.

"Birch Syrup" is for Glen and Melissa Simpson.

"Strong Stars" is for Melanie Montoya.

IV

"Across the Line": *Loteria* is a Mexican bingo game, with cards showing El Diablo (the devil), El Nopal (prickly pear), La Sirena (mermaid), and El Corazón (a biologically accurate heart pierced by an arrow). *Gordita*: a small, extra-thick corn tortilla formed like a shallow dish to hold vegetables, sauce, and meat. *Paletas*: fresh fruit Popsicles. *Piña*: pineapple. All of the tap water for the City of Tucson comes from underground reservoirs and rivers.

"Again, Again" owes its existence to the Rilke poem with the same title.

"Short History of One Hour's Desire":
Chicken scratch is a kind of music played by Tohono O'odham and Pima musicians in Arizona.

Mola is the name for the brightly colored, cut and layered cloth pictures made by the Kuna women on the San Blas Islands off Panama. The artists wear their work as clothing. Most collectors frame it.

Charango is a ten-string musical instrument crafted from the shell of an armadillo. *Cuíca* is a friction drum, often used in Brazilian music.

Día de los Muertos (Day of the Dead), a celebration of life, with a candlelight procession, vigils, feasts for the dead and the living, and La Mascarada, ritual dance with masks.

"Wide Icy River" is for Kip, Tito, Joaquín, and especially Lupita.

Peggy Shumaker

was born in La Mesa, California, in 1952. She grew up in Tucson and received her B.A. and M.F.A. from the University of Arizona. In 1989 she was awarded a National Endowment for the Arts Poetry Fellowship. For 1992–93 she was president of the Associated Writing Programs' Board of Directors. She teaches in the M.F.A. program at the University of Alaska Fairbanks and lives in a log house near Ester, Alaska.

PITT POETRY SERIES

Ed Ochester, General Editor

Archibald MacLeish, *The Great American Fourth
  of July Parade*
Peter Meinke, *Liquid Paper: New and Selected Poems*
Peter Meinke, *Night Watch on the Chesapeake*
Carol Muske, *Applause*
Carol Muske, *Wyndmere*
Leonard Nathan, *Carrying On: New & Selected Poems*
Ed Ochester and Peter Oresick, *The Pittsburgh Book of
  Contemporary American Poetry*
Sharon Olds, *Satan Says*
Alicia Suskin Ostriker, *Green Age*
Alicia Suskin Ostriker, *The Imaginary Lover*
Greg Pape, *Black Branches*
Greg Pape, *Storm Pattern*
Kathleen Peirce, *Mercy*
David Rivard, *Torque*
Liz Rosenberg, *Children of Paradise*
Liz Rosenberg, *The Fire Music*
Maxine Scates, *Toluca Street*
Richard Shelton, *Selected Poems, 1969–1981*
Betsy Sholl, *The Red Line*
Peggy Shumaker, *The Circle of Totems*
Peggy Shumaker, *Wings Moist from the Other World*
Jeffrey Skinner, *The Company of Heaven*
Leslie Ullman, *Dreams by No One's Daughter*
Constance Urdang, *Alternative Lives*
Constance Urdang, *Only the World*
Ronald Wallace, *The Makings of Happiness*
Ronald Wallace, *People and Dog in the Sun*
Belle Waring, *Refuge*
Michael S. Weaver, *My Father's Geography*
Robley Wilson, *Kingdoms of the Ordinary*
Robley Wilson, *A Pleasure Tree*
David Wojahn, *Glassworks*
David Wojahn, *Mystery Train*
Paul Zimmer, *Family Reunion: Selected and New Poems*